STANDARD GRADE HISTORY

CHANGE IN SCOTLAND 1830~1930

Wendy Doran

and

Richard Dargie

Chambers

Contents

CHAPTER ONE
Population in Scotland

More mouths to feed

IN THE 1830s, the population of Scotland was increasing. The number of Scots continued to grow until the 1920s. Each year there were more mouths to feed and more families needing clothes and housing.

These extra people caused problems which could not be solved overnight. Ways of producing more food had to be found. Overcrowded houses were common throughout this period.

The extra people also created a demand for products which led to new industries. Better ways of transporting goods also had to be developed.

To meet the needs of a growing population, Scotland had to change into a modern industrial country.

SOURCE A: The population of Scotland, 1821–1931

1821 – 2.09 million	1861 – 3.06 million	1901 – 4.47 million
1831 – 2.36 million	1871 – 3.36 million	1911 – 4.76 million
1841 – 2.62 million	1881 – 3.73 million	1921 – 4.88 million
1851 – 2.88 million	1891 – 4.02 million	1931 – 4.84 million

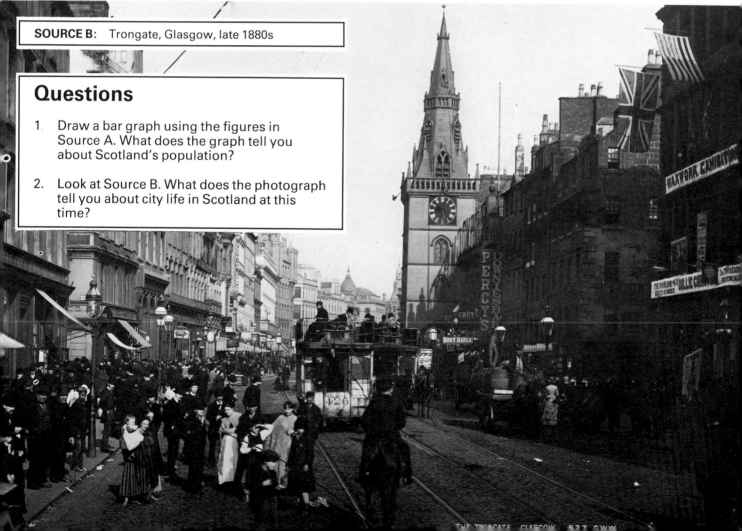

SOURCE B: Trongate, Glasgow, late 1880s

Questions

1. Draw a bar graph using the figures in Source A. What does the graph tell you about Scotland's population?

2. Look at Source B. What does the photograph tell you about city life in Scotland at this time?

People on the move

SOURCE C: *Aberdeen Evening Express* photograph, 'Flittin'

BETWEEN 1830 and 1930 there were great movements of people across Scotland. Families that had always lived in one place had to move as their old way of life disappeared.

For many hundreds of years the people of Scotland had been spread evenly across the land. Most Scots were peasants who made their living from their crops and animals. Many lived in the northern and western glens.

Lowland and coastal towns were small. Glasgow and Edinburgh, by far the largest cities, had only around 80 000 inhabitants each in 1801.

Though the total population rose throughout the nineteenth century, not all parts of the country saw a rise in numbers. The four main cities of Scotland grew rapidly, and in 1930 most towns were larger than they had been in 1830. By 1900 almost a million people lived in Glasgow, the second largest city in Britain then.

But many people were leaving country areas. New ways of farming often meant there was less work available for them to do. Many families lost their land. The young and the ambitious went in search of jobs and better wages in the towns. Village life slowly faded away.

Almost all of highland Scotland was deserted by the 1880s. Vast areas that had once been farmed were given over to sheep, deer and grouse. By the start of this century the majority of Scots lived in a narrow, crowded strip running across central Scotland and up the east coast.

Questions

1. Where do you think the people in Source C are moving to?

2. Suggest a reason why this family might be on the move.

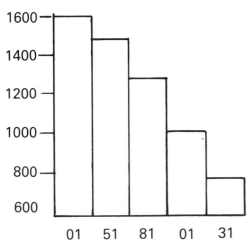

Strathdon (a country parish in Aberdeenshire),
1801–1931 (in hundreds)

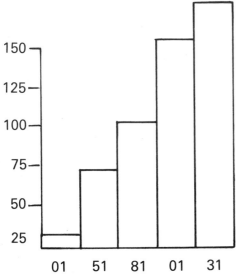

Aberdeen City Census, 1801–1931,
(in thousands)

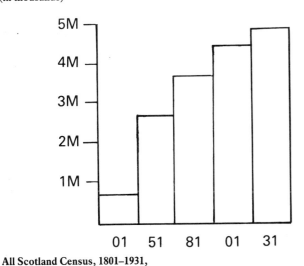

All Scotland Census, 1801–1931,
(in millions)

SOURCE D: Population changes from the National Census, 1801–1931

SOURCE E: Map showing where Scots moved between 1830 and 1930

Things to Do

1. Study Source D. Which of the following statements best describes what these graphs show?
    (a) The population in Scotland went up everywhere.
    (b) The population in Scotland overall and in cities went up but it fell in rural areas.
    (c) The population in Aberdeen was bigger than the population in Scotland as a whole.

2. Look at Source E.
    Match the arrows with the phrases below. Copy and rearrange the table.

Arrow number	Population movement
	Scots emigrating overseas throughout the period.
	Skilled Scots moving to England for jobs in the 1920s.
	Landless Highlanders looking for work in the Central Belt.
	Country people moving to work in the east coast towns.
	The influx of poor Irish to the Glasgow area after 1840.

An empty country

IN 1830 ALMOST half of Scotland's people still lived in the Highlands. But for 60 years, since the 1770s, many had been leaving for a new life in the south or overseas.

Gaelic became the second language of nineteenth-century Glasgow and there were over 15 million people of Scottish origin in North America by 1930.

Very many family homes in the Highlands had been abandoned. Villages and farms that had once been thriving became moor and wilderness again.

By 1930 much of northern Scotland had been cleared of people.

SOURCE F: The effects of emigration on a Highland village

Many of the people here have emigrated to America: many more are preparing to go to Australia. In some parts of this parish, where there was dense population 80 years ago, there are now to be found only a few scattered huts.

SOURCE G: New Statistical Account, Laggan, Inverness-shire

In 1826, all the people of the island of Rhum, amounting to 400 souls, found it necessary to leave their native country and seek new homes in the distant wilds of America. The old, to find tombs in a foreign land, the young to meet toils and dangers and become familiar with strange customs and habits. A similar emigration took place in 1828 from the island of Muck.

SOURCE H: New Statistical Account, Small Isles

Questions

1. Most Highlanders lived in simple houses like the ones shown in Source F; they owned few possessions.

   Why would this make them more likely to emigrate?

2. What evidence is there in Sources F, G and H to prove that parts of Scotland were being deserted?

3. Write down the name of the part of Scotland being described below:
   - 400 people emigrated from here to America in 1826.
   - Only a few scattered huts were left in this place.
   - Gaelic became the second language of this city.

4. What type of people would be more likely to leave Scotland. Young or old? Why?

5. Why is Source F a good source of evidence for Scottish emigration?

Why did so many leave?

IN SOME places the people were forced to go. The owners of the land, the lairds, wanted to make higher profits from their estates.

The lairds decided to let their land to sheep farmers from the south. Sheep were well suited to the hilly moors that cover much of the Highlands. But there was not enough grazing for sheep and the cattle of the local people. Often the choice for them was to emigrate, or stay and starve.

> *The decrease in this district is due to emigration caused by the introduction of sheep-farming to the partial exclusion of cattle . . .*

SOURCE I: Invermoriston, 1845

Many other tenant farmers were unable to pay the ever-rising rents and were forced from their homes. In the north of Scotland, in Sutherland, the Clearances were sometimes brutal and bitter.

> *Parties of Constables rushed on the houses of the people, and immediately began to set fire to them till about three hundred were in flames. Little or no time was given for the removal of persons or property. The people tried to remove the sick and the helpless before the fire should reach them . . .*

SOURCE J: Eye-witness Donald MacLeod, villager in Sutherland, 1819

Questions

1. Why might we be suspicious of Donald MacLeod's account of the Clearances?

2. Imagine you were being forced to leave your home in the Highlands. Write a letter to a cousin who is already in America saying why you are going to join him.

PUSHED OR PULLED?

SOURCE L: *Aberdeen Journal*, 1831

EMIGRATION
TO THE TOWN OF GAMBIER,
AND FERTILE SETTLEMENT OF OHIO,
NORTH AMERICA.

Trustees to Kenyon College and the Ohio Fund.
The Right Honourable Lord Kenyon.
The Right Honourable Lord Gambier.
The Right Honourable Lord Bexley.
George Wharton Mariott, Esq. B.C.L.

CAPITALISTS, AGRICULTURISTS, STUDENTS, MECHANICS, and others, EMIGRATING to this highly favoured SETTLEMENT, (or to any of the other STATES of AMERICA,) may receive every information, of the superior advantages which it possesses, secure their passage in first class American ships, and make arrangements for the occupation of Land, and purchase of the same, in any quantities, at the rate of ONE POUND, British, per acre, on application to the appointed Agent, CHARLES GALINDO.
Applications from the South of Scotland to be made to
DAVID SMITH,
Dock Gates, LEITH.
For the North of Scotland, to Mr GEO. MAITLAND, ELGIN.—*Unpaid Letters are not received.*

The Clearances continued right up to the 1880s. Many tenants chose to go after 1846 when the potato crop failed and there was famine across the Highlands. Some lairds had to spend great sums of money that year to keep the local people fed. It was often cheaper to pay their fare on a ship to a new land overseas.

After the railways came to Scotland some lairds wanted to introduce deer stalking and grouse shooting on their land. Such sport was not only fun, but attracted rich tourists to Scotland. The local people had to move again.

Questions

1. Which of the people shown in Source K do you think are local? Give a reason for your answer.

2. Many advertisements like Source L appeared in Scottish newspapers in the nineteenth century.
   (a) How does this advertisement try to make emigration to America seem a good idea?
   (b) Can the information in this advertisement be trusted? Explain your answer.

Other people left the country, not because they were pushed, but because they were pulled. Scotland has never been a rich country. Other lands offered the promise of cheap farmland, work for all and wealth. Right up to the present day, many skilled Scots have gone south to England or abroad in search of jobs.

> *Since 1831 numerous craftsmen and spinners have emigrated to the Continent, and in the spring of 1841 nearly a hundred carpenters left the port of Aberdeen to form a shipbuilding establishment in one of the North American colonies.*

SOURCE M: Census Note, 1841

SOURCE N: Canadian Emigration Office poster

Questions

1. Read Source M above. What kinds of people were leaving Scotland?

2. Look at Source N. Make a list of the things in the poster which would attract Scots to emigrate to Canada.

3. How do you think emigration affected Scotland?

Things to Do

1. Look at a map of North America. Find as many places with Scottish names as you can.

2. North America includes the USA as well as Canada. Design a poster similar to the one shown, which might attract Scots to the USA.

3. Survey the people in your class to find out how many of them have relatives in North America or Australia. Draw a bar graph to display your results.

The growing cities

AS IT became harder to make a living on the land, more Scots tried their luck in the growing towns. In 1801, only one in every ten Scots lived in a city. By 1901, more than a third, 36%, were city dwellers. Moving to Glasgow, Edinburgh, Aberdeen or Dundee offered many the chance of a job in a factory and a new way of life.

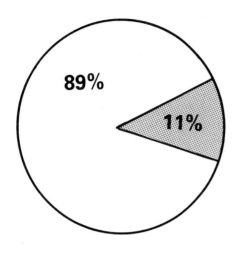

In 1801 only 11% of Scots lived in towns and cities.

> *The cause of the extraordinary increase in population is due to the great growth of the linen trade, which has produced so many spinning mills . . . By giving employment to thousands, it has encouraged early marriages, as well as bringing families from other parts of Scotland and from Ireland.*

SOURCE O: New Statistical Account, Dundee, 1833

> *The increase of the population may be explained by the ease with which even boys employed at weaving get possession of money; able to earn considerable wages before they had acquired sense to manage them, many hurried into matrimony; and their wives being equally young and thoughtless, they indulged in dress and luxuries, and preserved no portion of their gains.*

SOURCE P: New Statistical Account, Lesmahagow, 1834

> *The increase in population is owing to the coal works in the parish, and the nearby iron works.*

SOURCE Q: New Statistical Account, New Monkland, Airdrie, 1835

> *Since 1811, the population here has been greatly increasing, and the only way of accounting for it, is the extension of the Marquis of Lothian's colliery. For years past, there have been many more hands employed in it than at any former period.*

SOURCE R: New Statistical Account, Newbattle, 1839

> *19% of Dundee's population was by 1850 of Irish origin. By that date, 55% of female textile workers in the city were Irish girls living in lodgings.*

SOURCE S: Scottish Population Survey

Things to Do

1. Look at the pie chart showing the percentage of Scots living in towns in 1801.
   Draw a similar pie chart for 1901 using the information in the text.

2. Read Sources O, P, Q, R and S. Make a list of the reasons they give to explain why the towns and cities of Scotland were growing.

3. (a) Which of these sources passes comment on the population growth?
   (b) How would you describe the attitude of the writer to this growth?
   (c) Suggest a reason why the writer felt this way.

Why were there more people?

IN THE 1830s, a quarter of all babies died in their first year. In 1861, more than half the deaths in Glasgow were children younger than ten years old. Life expectancy was low.

Yet the population of Scotland grew each year between 1830 and 1920. People at the time gave many reasons for the rise in the numbers of people.

A better, varied diet led to stronger, healthier people. Medical knowledge improved greatly during the period. More people understood the link between filth and disease. Clean water was supplied to the towns and cities.

By 1930, many diseases that had once been common had vanished from Scotland. By 1930, the children of poor families had a much better chance of living to become healthy adults.

SOURCE T: New Statistical Account, Arbroath, 1833

Causes of death in Arbroath, 1828–1832

Consumption	198	Cramp	11
Age & decay	184	Teething	10
Water in head	50	Cancer	4
Hooping cough	49	Jaundice	3
Still-born	45	Complaint in head	3
Bowel complaint	44	Hysterical fits	2
Croup	41	Gravel	2
Fever	40	Mortification	2
Inflamation	31	Stomach complaint	2
Accidents	28	Vomiting of blood	2
Paralysis	23	Sore throat	1
Bowel hive	22	Exposure to cold	1
Dropsy	17	White-swelling	1
Inward complaint	17	Broken leg	1
Child-birth	16	Wound in the leg	1
Asthma	15	Untimely birth	1
Smallpox	15	Suicide	1
Measles	13	Not Stated	2

Total deaths 898

Things to Do

1. Look at Source T. It shows the main diseases in Scotland in 1832.
   (a) What is unusual about this list?
   (b) Make up a short list of the main diseases today. What differences between these two lists do you notice?

2. Use Sources T and U to explain why there were more people in Scotland in 1930 than in 1830.

SOURCE U: Number of burials in Arbroath, 1828–1832

Age 1 to 10 – 337	Age 50 to 60 – 48
Age 10 to 20 – 62	Age 60 to 70 – 100
Age 20 to 30 – 66	Age 70 to 80 – 92
Age 30 to 40 – 55	Age 80 to 90 – 68
Age 40 to 50 – 49	Age 90 to 99 – 8

Things to Investigate

1. Look back through this chapter.
   Look for sources that come from the New Statistical Account.
   Make a list of the things mentioned in these extracts.

2. Ask at your school or local library to see the New Statistical Account report on your area.
   (a) What has changed in your area since the 1830s?
   (b) Has anything survived down to the present day?
   (c) Can you see why the New Statistical Account is an important source for historians?

CHAPTER TWO
Life on the Land

Changes in farming

IN 1830 MOST people in Scotland still worked as farmers. But changes were taking place in agriculture which were beginning to alter life on the land.

Many Scots were finding that they could not afford to keep up small farms or crofts so they moved to the towns or coastal areas to find other kinds of work.

SOURCE A:
A deserted croft in Sutherland

In remote areas of the Highlands and Hebrides . . . lairds tried to make land more profitable by turning great tracts into sheep runs, clearing people from the islands and glens in the process.

SOURCE B: Ann Glen: *Contemporary Scotland – Farming*, 1975

In other areas, however, the picture was quite different. Those who had bigger farms were able to benefit from new farming methods and so improve their standard of living.

In this parish there used to be four or five sheep walks, but now the ground is under culture of the plough. The population of this county has increased considerably.

SOURCE C: G. Buchanan-Hepburn: *The Agriculture of East Lothian*, 1794

Questions

1. (a) In which parts of Scotland were people leaving their farms?
   (b) Give two reasons why they were leaving.

2. Name one area of Scotland where people were improving their farms. Why were they able to do this?

3. What is the difference between the changes in Source B and Source C? Can you think of a reason for this?

Bigger fields

MOST SCOTTISH landlords (lairds) wanted to make as much profit from the land as possible. They were interested in improvements which would help them to do this. They had, in the past, rented out small pieces of land (rigs) to tenant farmers for short periods of time. Now they began to let larger, enclosed fields to farmers who could pay higher rents. Their leases were longer too, so that they would have time to introduce the new improvements.

> Leases were usually for 19 years but 31 years was not uncommon. Some landlords specified the type of farming to be followed while others left the tenant a free hand. All took care to prevent the tenant from exhausting the land in the final years of the lease.

SOURCE D: James Handley: *The Agricultural Revolution in Scotland*

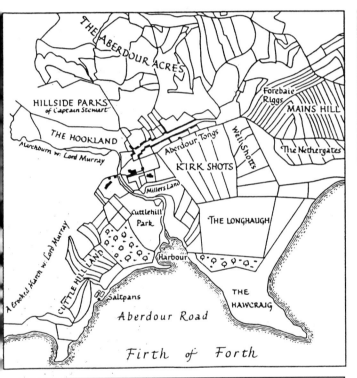

SOURCE E: The Estate of Aberdour, Fife, before enclosure

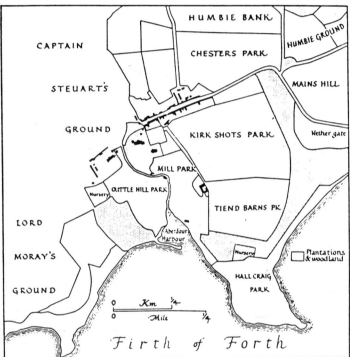

SOURCE F: The Estate of Aberdour, Fife, after enclosure

Questions

1. How long did the new leases last for?

2. According to Source D, what had been worrying the Scottish landlords? How might longer leases help to prevent this?

3. Compare Sources E and F. Write down a list of all the differences you can see in the two maps.

Better farms

WHAT WERE these farming 'improvements' which so many farmers were keen to use? These improvements included:

- buying machinery to speed up the jobs done on the farm;

- improving the quality of the soil, using fertilisers such as lime;

- growing root crops such as potatoes and turnips which provided winter food for animals and people. They also helped to put goodness back into the soil;

- rotating root crops with grain crops like wheat and oats. This improved the crop yield.

Livestock was also improved by careful feeding and breeding. Cattle breeds like the Aberdeen-Angus for beef and the Ayrshire for dairy products were developed. Scotland also became famous for its powerful Clydesdale horses, Galloway cattle and Blackface and Cheviot sheep.

Trees were planted to give shelter and protection to both crops and livestock.

Scottish roads were improved too. This meant that the farmer could now get his produce to market more easily.

SOURCE G: Double Horse and Cart, *Stephen's Book of the Farm*, 1855

Things to Do

1. Write down the farming improvement which matches each description below:

   Sheltered crops and animals ....

   Speeded up the work ....

   Provided winter food ....

   Improved the soil ....

2. Look at Source G. Do you think this farmer is doing well? Write down the improvements you think he has been able to introduce and benefit from.

Ploughing

ONE OF the farming jobs which changed most during the period 1830–1930 was ploughing. This is the method by which the earth is dug and turned over to prepare it for planting. On small farms or crofts it was often done by hand, using a cas chrom or foot plough.

SOURCE H:
Crofters on Skye using the cas chrom, c.1920

On larger farms a new, lightweight metal plough was used. It could plough the bigger fields more quickly.

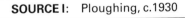

SOURCE I: Ploughing, c.1930

This plough may look clumsy to use, but it worked very well. The nets over the horses were to keep flies off them.

Questions

1. Look at Source H. Why do you think these crofters were still using the cas chrom in 1920?

2. This photograph was published in a book for farmers in the 1930s. Why do you think the photograph was published? How would this type of plough help the farmer?

Harvesting

IN 1830 CORN was still cut with a sickle and threshed with a flail. Both tasks were done by hand so farms required a great number of workers at harvest time. It was a good time for unemployed men and women to find work. Children were also able to lend a hand, tying the corn into sheaves.

> The scythe . . . was not used then in cutting crop, only the 'heuk' (sickle) being used. In 'heuk cutting' the crop was cut in handfuls, and laid on the bands till the desired quantity was gathered. A binder came after who twisted the straw bands into a firm knot . . . The sheaves were not set up in stooks then, but stood singly in rows on the field.

SOURCE J: John Firth: *Reminiscences of an Orkney Parish*, 1850

By the turn of the century, however, many farms had started to use mechanical reapers and binders which reduced the amount of labour required. These were usually powered by horses. Only a few farms in Scotland used steam power or tractors before 1930.

> 'Of course it was the reaper before the binder came on the scene. The ones I knew cut a four feet cut. There were three plain blades and the fourth had taes that pulled off the sheaf and you had to make bands to tie it and you had to get it out of the road fast. The binder was a great advance. It puts the bands on and left the sheaf ready to stook. There were ten sheaves in a stook.'

SOURCE K: Reminiscences of a farm worker in Aberdeenshire, c.1920

Things to Do

1. Do you think Sources J and K are reliable? Give a reason for your answer.

2. Write a paragraph headed 'Harvesting Corn'. Describe the differences between doing this job in 1830 and doing the same job in 1920. You should mention:
   (a) the tools or machinery used,
   (b) the number of people needed,
   (c) the amount of time it might take.

SOURCE L: Reaping, c.1920

Jobs on the farm

*M*ANY JOBS on Scottish farms were still done by hand in the 1920s.

Farmers needed a large workforce for harvesting the potato crop and seasonal labour was usually hired. The potatoes had to be sorted and graded by hand. The summer is short in Scotland and all farm jobs had to be done quickly. 'Make hay while the sun shines' is an old farming expression. Haymaking was also done by hand at this time.

Questions

1. Look at Sources M and N. Describe the jobs being done in these photographs.

2. Why is this type of job called 'seasonal'?

3. How would the use of manual labour help:
   (a) the farmer?
   (b) the local people?

4. Doing farm work used to be a good way to make friends. What evidence for this do you see in Sources M and N?

SOURCE N: Haymaking at Muirfield Farm, East Lothian

Hard times

THE GOLDEN age of farming in Scotland lasted from 1850 to 1870. As the towns grew, there were ever more mouths to feed. During this time farmers and lairds prospered and crop yields were high.

However, Scotland has also seen some hard times. In the 1870s, Scots started to buy more foreign food. Food prices at home began to fall and the income of Scottish farmers began to drop. Farm workers had to be laid off. The next 20 years were ones of unemployment and depression in the countryside. Thousands of families had to leave the rural areas and look for work in the towns.

Another wet August this year. A cold, wet, windy month. Corn battered badly in the fields. Wheat and barley very poor quality. Pastures on clay land are flooded like winter. Grass all trodden away and the cattle sunk in to their knees.

SOURCE O: *Scottish Farming Record*, 1879

The railway and the steamship are British inventions, but they have been used to damage this country. American business-men can now transport wheat from the great plains of Iowa and Kansas . . . across the Atlantic. And it is cheaper on the quays of Glasgow than the corn grown here.

SOURCE P: A Scottish newspaper report, 1878

Life on the farm was often difficult and uncomfortable. Wealthy farmers had large, well-furnished houses, but poorer farmers lived in cottages. Farm workers lived in bothies.

'The bothy just had a bed in it and a basin for washing – you had to carry all your water. If there were three or four of you, you might have two or three rooms of a bothy. In the south they sometimes had to cook for themselves and gey rough it could be, but hereabouts you fed in the farmhouse and the skivvy from the farm made your beds while you were out at work.'

SOURCE Q: Reminiscences of a farm worker, Aberdeenshire, 1920s

Questions and Things to Do

1. Look at Sources O and P. Write down three reasons why Scottish farming suffered in the 1870s.

2. Why was there so much unemployment in rural areas at this time?

3. In what ways was the life on a farm difficult and uncomfortable?

Farming and the First World War

IN 1914 BRITAIN went to war with Germany. The war lasted until 1918. Now farming became important again in Britain. It was a vital part of Britain's war effort. Vast armies had to be fed. The workers in the factories also needed a steady supply of food.

In 1916 Germany began to sink merchant ships carrying food into Britain. A war at sea developed, as the German U-boats tried to starve Britain into surrender. Seventy per cent of Britain's food was imported from abroad. If the supply lines at sea were cut, Britain could no longer fight.

Thousands of farm workers left the land in the first few weeks of the war and joined the army.

IMPORTS OF FOOD INTO BRITAIN IN 1914	
Meat	40% of national consumption
Cereals	80% of national consumption
Fruit	85% of national consumption
Sugar	100% of national consumption

SOURCE R: Government figures, 1914

Things to investigate

1. Look in your library for a map of your area or region. Draw or trace the map, shading in the farming areas. Find out what kind of farming is done there;
    e.g. sheep farming,
          dairy farming,
          arable farming,
          poultry farming.

2. Look in your kitchen at home to see what Scottish foodstuffs your family eats. Make a list of these and compare it to the foreign foods you eat.

3. Look at extracts 6 and 7 of the Scottish Film Council video *A Century of Change* (Section 1). What do they tell you about farm life before 1930? Look at extracts 1–3 from Section 3. What changes have taken place in agriculture this century?

4. Visit a local farm and find out what kind of farming tools and machines are used.

SOURCE S: A poster published during the war

'*Two young women dressed themselves up in green jerseys and tight breeches and went off to work on the land. Everyone was shocked by this tomboyish behaviour. Wearing men's trousers was regarded as the height of indecency.*'

SOURCE T: Oral Memory

Questions and Things to Do

1. Look at Source R.
    Draw a bar graph showing the amount of food imported into Britain in 1914. Which of these foods was not produced at all in Britain?

2. Look at Source S.
    (a) Who do you think published this poster?
    (b) Why do you think it was published?
    (c) How would this help the war effort?

3. Who went to help out on the farms during the war?

4. Which of the foods listed in Source R do you think Scottish farms were able to grow more of during the war?

CHAPTER THREE

The March of Industry

People at work

BEFORE 1830, most people in Scotland lived and worked on the land as farmers or farm labourers.

After 1830, more and more Scots worked in textile factories, coal mines and iron foundries. Scotland was becoming an industrial country.

Most of these new industries grew up in the Central Belt of Scotland.

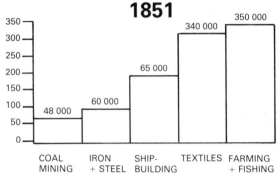

1851

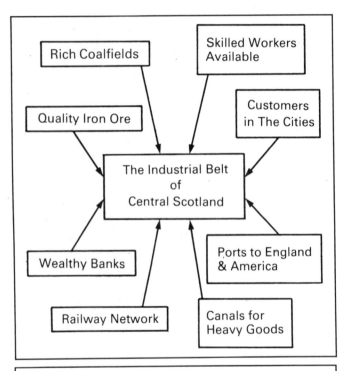

SOURCE A: Central Scotland

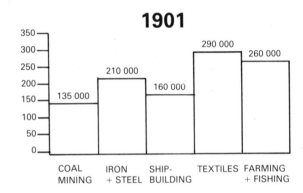

Workers in Scottish Industries, 1851 and 1901 (in thousands)

SOURCE B: Bar graphs of workers in 1851 and 1901

In order to keep working, people often had to learn new skills. They also had to move to those towns where there was work.

During the nineteenth century people moved from job to job as new industries sprang up and new machines were invented. Making cloth was the first industry which employed large numbers of workers in factories in Scotland. Gradually, however, more labourers were needed in the heavy industries such as coalmining and iron manufacture.

Questions

1. Using the diagram, Source A, explain why most of Scotland's industry was in the Central Belt.

2. Look at the bar graphs (Source B).
   (a) What were the main industries in 1851?
   (b) How had things changed by 1901?

3. Where would the extra workers for these industries have come from?

Power from the pit

IN THE nineteenth century coal was king. There was a huge demand for this fuel. Everyone wanted to burn coal to heat their homes. The new railway companies used it to power their trains. At every port great piles of coal were loaded aboard the steamers and puffers that were replacing sailing ships.

Cotton factories made cloth on looms that were linked to steam engines heated by coal. Coal was turned into coke to smelt iron in the great furnaces of Airdrie and Coatbridge. After 1860 it was also needed to make steel. By 1830, in many towns, streets and homes were lit by a burning flicker of coal-gas. Everything in Scotland ran on coal.

Thousands of families made their living from coal. The new industries and the fast-growing towns were all built above coalfields. Coal was the basis of the Scottish economy. By 1900 British mines were producing a staggering 230 million tons of coal each year.

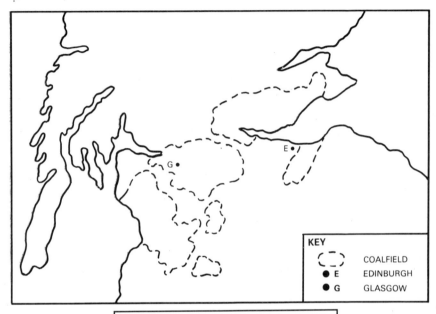

KEY

- - - COALFIELD
- E EDINBURGH
- G GLASGOW

SOURCE C: Coalfields in Scotland

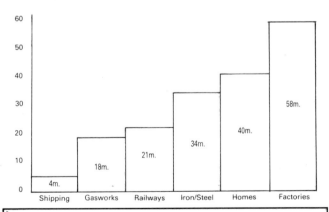

4m.	Shipping
18m.	Gasworks
21m.	Railways
34m.	Iron/Steel
40m.	Homes
58m.	Factories

SOURCE D: The demand for coal, 1900, in millions of tons

Things to Do

1. List the reasons why there was a great demand for coal after 1830.

2. Copy Source C. Using an atlas, mark on your map at least ten of the largest towns in Central Scotland.
   What do you notice on your copy of the map?

3. (a) Copy Source D. Mark on your copy of the table which of these users wanted coal as:
   (i) an energy source,
   (ii) a heating fuel,
   (iii) a raw material.

   (b) Which of these uses would provide jobs for the Scottish economy?

Problems in the pits

IN 1700 THERE had been places in Scotland where coal could be picked up on the earth's surface. As more coal was used, however, miners had to dig deeper underground. By 1850 most Scottish mines were over 1000 feet deep.

The deeper a mine went, the more dangerous it was to work in. The air underground was soon used up and became stale. Water seeped into the shafts and flooded the workings. Falling rock and cave-ins were common. There were explosive gases such as methane. Sparks lit floating clouds of coal dust which turned into fireballs. Winding gear to get workers and coal up from the pit was primitive.

Pit workers complained that the work was slow and hard. The coal was hacked out with picks and shovels by the sheer strength of the miners. Pit owners complained that the work was slow and expensive. The coal was often carried to the surface in baskets by women, or pulled up in small trucks.

Quicker and safer ways of working were needed to meet the growing demand for coal.

SOURCE F: In a pit shaft

SOURCE E: In an early nineteenth-century coal mine

The penitent, or fire man igniting the fire damp

Deaths by Gas Suffocation	4
Deaths by Drowning	6
Deaths in Fires	23
Deaths in Shafts	116
Deaths by Coal Wagons	187
Deaths in Cave-ins	312
Deaths in Gallery Explosions	405

SOURCE G: Table of deaths in British mines in 1910

Things to Do

1. Study Source E carefully. It shows an early miner. He is wearing wet rags and a hood. Suggest a reason for this, and explain what he is doing.

2. (a) What is happening in Source F?
   (b) What do you think was the original purpose of this picture? (Why was it drawn?)

3. (a) What were the main types of accident in coal mines in 1910?
   (b) Suggest a reason why this list of accidents was drawn up.
   (c) Who do you think drew up this list?

New technology

AT THE start of the nineteenth century all the jobs in a coal mine were done by hand. Families worked together, cutting, gathering and carrying coal to the surface by hand.

After 1850 new methods and machines were developed to speed up production. At first, ponies were used to drag the coal wagons to the surface. Later, steam engines did this, as well as winding the men up and down in safety cages. Railways carried the cut coal to market.

Extractor fans and pumps were used to suck up stale air, water and dangerous coal dust. Special dynamites were used to blast coal safely. The Davy Safety Lamp, invented in 1815, gave light to miners and lessened the chance of sparking a gas fire. Caged canaries were used to warn of poisonous gas.

Electric cutting machines had appeared in some mines by the early 1890s, but in many Scottish pits in 1920 much of the work was still done by hand-pick.

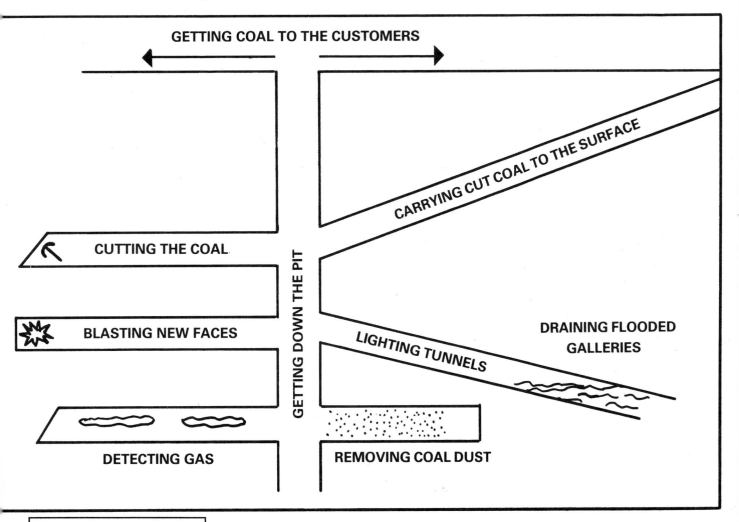

SOURCE L: Mining tasks

Things to Do

1. List the mining tasks shown in Source L. Use the information above to say how new technology affected each of these tasks.

Wages

IN SPITE of the harsh living and working conditions, Scottish working men continued to be attracted to coal mining.

This may have been because the jobs were secure – right up to the 1930s mining was a growth industry and redundancies were rare. It may also have been because the wages were slightly better than in other industries. In 1852, for example, a coal miner could expect to earn 28 shillings a week, compared to the 21 shillings that a factory worker earned. He was also given free coal to heat his house.

Nevertheless, the miner was dependent on the coal company he worked for and could not leave his job, even if he wanted to. His house was rented from the company and the local shop where he bought his food was owned by the coal company. Prices at the company shop were usually very high, but the miner could lose his job if he did not use it.

SOURCE M: Miners' cottages at Allanton, near Hamilton, c.1910

A miner's wages could be held back by his employer to pay his debts at the company shop, even though the man's wife and children were depending on his earnings. There was a great temptation to the man to spend his wages on drink . . . or to desert his family.

SOURCE N: Report on the Mining Population in Scotland, 1852

It is always understood that when a man leaves his work he and his family must remove from the house or 'flit', as it is called.

SOURCE O: Report of the Commissioners on Coal Mines, 1842

Questions

1. Look at Source M. Do you think these miners' families had a good standard of living? Give a reason for your answer.

2. Study Source N. Why do you think there was a great temptation for the miners to spend their wages on drink?

3. Imagine you were the son or daughter of a coal miner in the mid-nineteenth century. Write a few sentences describing the kind of life you have. What would happen to you if your father deserted the family?

Making iron

IRON IS made from iron ore which is dug from the ground by miners and then melted in a furnace until the iron runs out of the ore. Ironworks grew up in Scotland near coal mines because plentiful supplies of coal were needed for the furnaces.

The great manufacture of this parish is the iron trade. Nearly the whole population, with the exception of a few farmers and weavers and other necessary tradesmen, are employed in the coal and iron trade. There is no great town in the parish, but many of the villages are increasing daily. The centre of the parish, about Langlone and Coatbridge, is one large village.

SOURCE P: The Parish of Old Monkland, New Statistical Account, 1845

SOURCE Q: A Coatbridge iron furnace

Most of the ironstone was at one time obtained from pits in the neighbourhood, but now it has to be brought from a distance of from two to twenty miles. A complete system of railways connects the pits with the works. A great proportion of the manufactured iron is sent out by Monklands Canal.

SOURCE R: Gartsherrie ironworks, Lanarkshire, New Statistical Account, 1845

Questions

1. Look at Source P.
   (a) What were the main occupations in Coatbridge in 1845?
   (b) Why do you think the population of Coatbridge was 'increasing daily'?

2. Look at Sources Q and R.
   (a) What was the main means of transport for the iron industry?
   (b) According to Source R, why was a good form of transport necessary at the Gartsherrie ironworks?

3. Where do you think the iron from Gartsherrie and Coatbridge was going? What would it be used for?

Industry this century

DURING the nineteenth century, coal developed from a small industry to become the most important industry in Scotland. Coal powered the machinery of the factories, the furnaces of the iron-works, the steam engines of the railways and the ships which carried Scotland's exports all over the world.

Iron provided the basic material for all these products. The development of the coal and iron industries changed the Central Belt of Scotland from a mainly farming region to a thriving industrial area. It also caused Glasgow to grow as a port and trading centre.

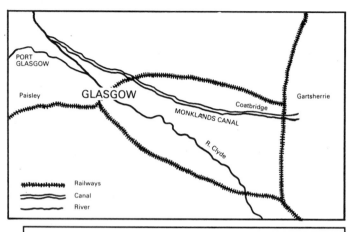

SOURCE S: Glasgow and surrounding area

Political rivalry with Germany led, from 1906, to a naval armaments race and many of the Dreadnoughts, the new all-big-gun ships, were Clyde-built. The Clyde yards also profited from the demand for merchant ships and luxury liners for crossing the Atlantic. Shipbuilding had become Scotland's key industry, for busy yards meant increased orders in coal mines, steel works, engineering shops and other industries.

SOURCE T: George Pryde: *Scotland 1603 – Present,* 1962

Things to Do

1. Copy out the statement below which best describes Scotland's industry at the start of this century:

   Shipbuilding had become more important than coal.

   Shipbuilding depended on the other heavy industries.

   Shipbuilding depended on rivalry with Germany.

2. Study Source T.
   (a) Name three types of ship which were built on the Clyde.
   (b) Explain how shipbuilding helped Scotland's other industries.

3. Design a poster dated 1906 to encourage people to come to Glasgow to work. Make use of the information given in Sources S and T.

Things to Investigate

1. Look for a map of Scotland which shows the mineral deposits (coal, iron, etc.). Copy the map and make a note of all the industries in Scotland which were dependent on these deposits.

2. Find out what the main industries of your area were during the period 1830–1930. How important to Scotland's economy are these industries today?

3. Interview an older person who worked in heavy industry before 1930. Record or transcribe the interview. Write one or two paragraphs about his or her working conditions, wages, hours of work, etc. How have heavy industries changed since that time?

CHAPTER FOUR
Railways

Carrying heavy goods

AS INDUSTRY developed, faster and better ways of carrying heavy goods were needed. Coal had to be taken from the mines to the towns. At first most people who had heavy goods to move sent them by water. Horses and wagons were used by mine and factory owners to get their goods to the canal or river. To speed up this form of transport rails were laid to ease the load the horse had to pull.

The rails of these early wagonways were made of wood, so they wore out quickly. The development of the iron industry in Scotland meant that iron rails could be used, and by 1830 all rails were made of iron. By then steam locomotives were being used to pull the wagons.

SOURCE A: A coal wagon on rails

One of the longest wagonways in Scotland was the Kilmarnock and Troon built in 1812 which measured 12 miles (19km). It was not only the first Scottish railway authorised by Act of Parliament but also the first to use a steam

Questions

1. Look at Source A. What technological development is being used here? Who would benefit from this?

Laying the lines

MOST OF Scotland's main railway lines were laid very quickly, between 1830 and 1850. But it was not easy work and many railway companies had building problems, for example:

- Iron rails were expensive.

- Extra workers were needed to lay the lines.

- Tunnelling through Scotland's hillsides was difficult and dangerous. Explosives were used, but much of the digging was done by candle and torch-light. Foul air and lack of ventilation made it uncomfortable for the workmen. Flooding was a problem too.

- Embankments and viaducts had to be built across valleys.

- Marsh and bog land presented problems. Floating rafts were made from heather and bracken and the lines laid on top.

- Stations had to be built with raised platforms for safety. In the early days of railways, many passengers were killed or injured crossing the lines.

Things to Do

1. Write down the problems experienced by:
   - (a) the railway companies,
   - (b) the workmen,
   - (c) the passengers.

2. Look at Source C. What dangers to workmen has the artist shown in this drawing?

SOURCE C: Building a viaduct over the River Ayr, c.1848

SOURCE D: The opening of the Glasgow-Garnkirk Railway, 1831

The railway navvies

EXTRA WORKMEN were needed to build the railways. They were called 'navvies' because other workers like them who had helped to build the canals had earned the name 'navigators'. Many of these men were Irish immigrants who had come to Scotland looking for work in the 1840s during the Irish famine. They carried picks and shovels and hired themselves out to the railway companies for work.

They made their home where they got their work. Some slept in huts constructed of damp turf, cut from wet grass, too low to stand upright. If they caught a fever, they died. Living like brutes, they were depraved, degraded and reckless. Drunkenness and low morale prevailed.

SOURCE F: Francis: *A history of the English Railway*

SOURCE E: An Irish railway navvy

The builders are tempted to adopt the cheapest method of working, without any regard to the danger to which the men will be exposed. Life is now recklessly sacrificed; needless misery . is inflicted. Innocent women and children are left widows and orphans. Such evils must not be allowed to continue, even though it be profitable.

SOURCE G: A newspaper report, 1846

Questions

1. How did the building of railways help the employment situation?

2. Look at Source E. What items did the railway navvy carry with him?

3. Compare Sources F and G. Which of these writers seems to be more sympathetic to the railway navvies? Choose words or phrases from the passage to support your answer.

Growth of the Scottish Railways

BY 1850 ONE THOUSAND miles of railways had been built in Scotland and new lines continued to be opened year by year. Railway lines were built using money borrowed from the general public. During the 1840s there was a 'Railway Mania' in Britain; people expected to make large sums of money from the success of the railway companies. Landowners started to raise the price of their land and this made rail fares high.

Ayr – Glasgow	1840
Greenock – Glasgow	1841
Kilmarnock – Glasgow	1841
Leith – Edinburgh	1841
Edinburgh – Glasgow	1842
London – Edinburgh	1846
London – Glasgow	1850
Glasgow – Aberdeen	1850

SOURCE H: Railway lines opened in Scotland, 1840–1850

Things to Do

1. Look at Source H. Which two towns were most railway lines built to and from? Can you think of a reason for this?

2. Study Source I. What extra expense would the North British Railway Company have in building its line from Edinburgh to Aberdeen?

3. Copy or trace the map into your notebook. Mark each railway line in a different colour.
   (a) Which line do you think would be used most?
   (b) Which line would have been nearest to your home?
   (c) Why are the Scottish islands not shown on this map?

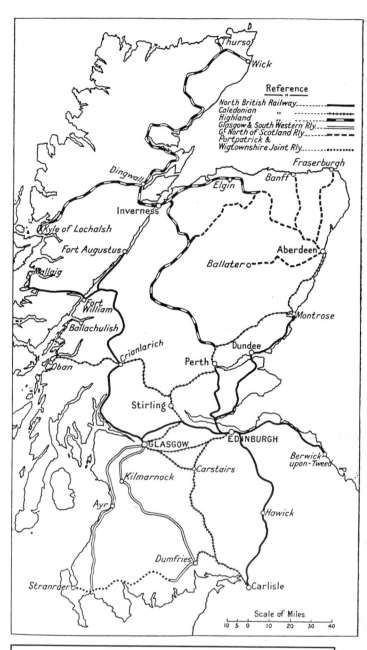

SOURCE I: Railways in Scotland before 1921

Cheap travel

UNTIL 1840 travel by rail was expensive, so only the rich could afford to take the train. Some railway companies then started to reduce their fares to encourage more people to travel by rail. In 1844 a law was passed which said that each new railway line was to provide at least one train a day in each direction.

This train was to stop at all stations and charge passengers not more than one penny a mile in third-class coaches. Seats 'protected from the weather' had to be provided. This law meant that ordinary working people could now afford to travel by train.

A young woman will hand over her box of clothes to the porter, get her ticket for Glasgow, pull on her gloves, laugh and talk with her parents and comrades, jump into the train, wave her handkerchief and thank her stars that she is at last leaving the unwomanly job [farm work] for domestic service and town society.

SOURCE J: Adapted from Evidence to a Royal Enquiry

Questions

1. Read Source J. Does the passage describe
   (a) an upper-class lady?
   (b) an ordinary working girl?
   (c) a middle-class housewife?
   Explain how the railway made it possible for her to leave home like this.

2. Study Source K.
   (a) What benefits do you think the penny train would have for Scotland's workers?
   (b) What would be the disadvantages of travelling by this train?
   (c) What kind of occupations do you think the people in the picture have?

SOURCE K: Trains for the poor; a workmen's penny train, 1865

Objections to railways

NOT EVERYONE liked the new railways. Canal companies, stagecoach owners and roadbuilders had most to lose. They were afraid the railways would put them out of business. But some other objections were ridiculous.

SOURCE L:
Objections to railways

Things to Do

1. Study Sources L and M. Now copy this chart

'Doon the Watter'

SOURCE S: The Broomielaw, c.1900

STEAM ENGINES were used to power ships as well as locomotives. Travel by steam ship remained popular with the people of Scotland, even after the coming of the railways. Steam ships sailed along canals, up and down rivers, and between islands. They carried goods as well as passengers. A trip 'doon the water' to resorts like Rothesay, Millport or Largs was a popular excursion for those in Glasgow. Further north, steam ships were available on many routes: to the Western Isles, along the Caledonian Canal and across the Pentland Firth to Orkney.

Questions

1. Look at Source S. What kinds of people do you think went on this type of excursion? Where do you think they went?

2. Now look at Source T.
   (a) What method of transport are these people using?
   (b) What kind of people are they?
   (c) Where do you think they are going?

SOURCE T: A picture postcard, 1904

Things to Investigate

1. Look at the Ordnance Survey map for your area. If there is a railway marked, make a list of the things the railway companies built for this line, e.g. bridges, stations, embankments, etc.

2. Interview an older person (grandparent, elderly neighbour or relative) to find out how they travelled to work, spent their days off or went on holiday when they were young. How has travelling changed since then?

CHAPTER FIVE
Health and Housing

City slums

SCOTLAND'S cities grew quickly in the nineteenth century. Workers and their families flooded in from the countryside, the Highlands, and from famine-stricken Ireland. They came looking for jobs in the new industries that were springing up in the towns.

At first, few new houses were built for these incomers. They had to find a place to live in the old rotting quarters of the cities. Buildings where the rich used to live were split into tiny one- and two-roomed flats.

After 1830 some new tenements were built for factory workers. They were built quickly and cheaply. There were few facilities and little privacy. The result was overcrowding, poverty and disease. For much of this period, many Scots lived in conditions that were hardly fit for humans.

SOURCE A: Women at an Edinburgh tenement well, 1924

Dr Keith gave evidence and said; 'The crowding is fearful. I have seen seven or eight sleeping in one tiny room, and have more than once been nearly suffocated on entering an apartment . . .'

SOURCE B: Report on the Sanitary Condition of the Aberdeen Poor, 1840

Houses in Scotland with one room *34%*
Houses in Scotland with two rooms *37%*

SOURCE C: National Census for 1861

Things to Do

1. Copy the following statements. Complete them, using as much of the information given above as possible.
   (a) Slum dwellers often came from ....
   (b) Many Scottish families lived in ....
   (c) We know there was no air in some tenements because ....
   (d) One source that tells us about housing then is ....

2. Write down three daily problems the women in Source A would have had to deal with because they had no inside water supply.

3. Use Source C to make a bar graph that shows the percentage of Scottish houses in the mid-nineteenth century that had:
   only one room;
   only two rooms;
   three or more rooms.

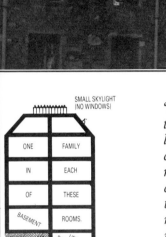

'The basement rooms are up to 14 feet below the street level. The tiny attic rooms are stuffy in summer, miserable in winter, and awkward in shape. All of the rooms are small and narrow. The end of the bed is often cut off, so the family is unable to lie at full length.'

SOURCE E: Cross-section of a Scottish tenement with lower basement, 1860

In a building of 59 rooms, there live 248 people in 56 families. The building is damp, unhealthy and rat-infested. In this huge warren, there is no water, no water-closet, no sink. There is nowhere to keep a refuse pail, or to keep food except in a chest of drawers. Many rooms have no bed, the family sleeping on straw, and measure only five feet and six inches from floor to ceiling.

SOURCE G: Report on the Conditions of the Poorer Classes of Edinburgh, 1868

'The bedclosets are a cause of much ill-health. These open away from any fresh air currents, and are a breeding ground for vermin. The back rooms are dark, so the tenant is forced to burn gas all day at great expense.'

SOURCE F: Floor plan of a tenement flat, Edinburgh, 1925

Things to Do

1. Look carefully at Source D. What problems would the people living in these tenements have?

2. Look at Sources E and F. List the dangers to health that you can see in these houses.

3. Look at Sources F and G. Note the measurements in these sources.
   Use them to measure out the size of a tenement room. What would it be like to live in a room that size?

4. Why do you think Sources B and G were written?

Courts, wynds and alleyways

SCOTLAND'S main towns and cities were founded in the Middle Ages. The streets were dark narrow lanes called wynds. At the end of each wynd was a close, an open court about 15–20 feet square, closed in by high tenements. In the centre of the court was the midden or dunghill where dirt, rubbish and sewage were collected.

Sometimes these wynds were many hundreds of years old. The buildings were often very decayed. There were few drains or sewers in these stinking places.

Before the 1860s, Town Councils had little authority to plan where streets ran or houses were built. Private builders could buy land and do with it as they pleased. Houses were built alongside with factories and slaughterhouses.

SOURCE H: A Scottish city street, 1925

The corporation of Skinners had a range of tan-pits supplied by filthy water from a burn in the middle of a narrow street, and the slaughterhouse was placed here . . . The dung of the slaughterhouse and the intestines of slaughtered animals were collected in heaps and allowed to rot for months . . .

SOURCE J: New Statistical Account, Glasgow, 1845

'A few old men sweep the streets, but sometimes the sweepings remain on the pavements for many days; the refuse from the gaol is flung down the 'sivers' creating the most offensive odours; the slaughterhouse being at the top of the town, the blood from it is allowed to flow down the main street . . .'

SOURCE I: Report on Conditions in Stirling, 1842

Things to Do

1. Study Source H.
    What does this source tell you about city streets and houses in 1925?

2. Why do you think people were prepared to put up with the conditions described in Sources I and J?

3. Look at a street plan of the town or city nearest to you.
    Look for evidence of the wynds and courts that made up the old street plan.

King Cholera

THE STREETS and houses of Scotland's cities were overcrowded. There was little fresh water, poor ventilation and few street gutters, drains or sewers. These conditions led to diseases like typhus, tuberculosis and the most feared killer of the age – cholera.

There were three great cholera epidemics in 1832, 1848 and 1853. Thousands of Scots died from this violent and painful disease. Thousands more were terrified, for no-one knew how the infection was caused or spread; some thought it was due to something bad in the air. Some rich people said that cholera was sent by God to punish the poor.

When the disease first struck Scotland in 1832, few people suspected that these horrible deaths were caused by the filth in the streets mixing with the drinking water supply of so many Scottish families.

This was the year of the Cholera – a disease which carried off many individuals, particularly females of the manufacturing population, who are doomed to damp workshops, stooping postures, meagre fare and long hours.

SOURCE L: New Statistical Account, Hamilton, 1832

Cholera showed itself in the city on the 12th February 1832 and continued until the 11th November. During that period there were 6208 cases and 3005 deaths. In the first outbreak, poorly fed persons who were dwelling in the crowded ill-aired parts of the city, were chiefly affected.

The second outbreak was more severe, the attacks scattered over the town. Many healthy persons, in comfortable circumstances, fell victims to the disease.

SOURCE M: New Statistical Account, Glasgow, 1835

THE POOR MAN'S FRIEND.

SOURCE K: Cartoon from *Punch*, 'The Poor Man's Friend'

Things to Do

1. Look at Source K. This cartoon was entitled 'The Poor Man's Friend'.
   (a) What does the cartoon show?
   (b) What point do you think the artist was trying to make?

2. Look at Sources L and M.
   (a) Name three groups of people who caught cholera in Glasgow in 1832.
   (b) What reasons are given in the sources to explain why people got this disease?

3. Use the books in your school library to find out more about cholera.
   Find out what caused it, how it was spread, what the symptoms were and how it was eventually controlled.

Fighting the fever

GRADUALLY medical knowledge improved and public action was taken against disease.

Local Boards of Health were set up when cholera broke out. These Boards could quarantine a town from incoming ships or travellers that might be infected. They had the power to close and fumigate infected buildings, and to open fever wards in local hospitals. Inns and lodging houses were examined regularly so that infected bedding could be burned.

Town Councils began to fight the causes of these fevers. Street scavengers were paid to remove any filth from public places. Soup kitchens were set up in poor areas to help feed the weakest. New deeper graveyards were dug, often on the edge of towns, to bury the victims. The wealthy had to pay a rate or tax towards these public health improvements.

SOURCE N: Albion Street Cholera Hospital, Glasgow, 1832			
February	40 patients	33 dead	7 cured
March	97 patients	69 dead	28 cured
April	122 patients	81 dead	41 cured
May	56 patients	40 dead	16 cured
June	126 patients	94 dead	32 cured
July	240 patients	143 dead	97 cured
August	273 patients	176 dead	97 cured
September	64 patients	33 dead	31 cured

The cholera has returned to the same streets, houses and rooms which it attacked in 1832. In Pollockshaws, it has snatched its first victim from the same room and the very bed in which it broke out in 1832. In Leith, the disease has struck hardest in the same rooms where it raged twenty years before.

SOURCE O: The *Edinburgh Review*, 1852

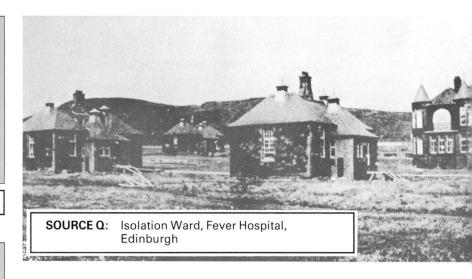

SOURCE Q: Isolation Ward, Fever Hospital, Edinburgh

The District Surgeons believe that cholera is most common where a lack of cleanliness is observable, particularly in the narrow lanes which prevent the circulation of free air. It will be the duty of the Board of Health to enforce public cleanliness in these wynds and courts by removing all nuisances and by whitewashing and liming them.

SOURCE P: *Aberdeen Journal*, 1840

Things to Do

1. Study Source N.
   (a) At which time of year was the disease at its strongest?
   (b) Suggest a reason why this was the case.

2. Study Source O. What would the events in Pollockshaws and Leith suggest to doctors who were looking for the cause of cholera?

3. What action was taken against the disease, according to Source P?

4. What clue is there in Source Q which tells you that these are fever wards for infectious patients?

Why were the slums so bad?

1. The town centres were old, and had not been planned properly. They were not meant to house the great numbers of people that were moving into them in the early nineteenth century. By 1830, many of the buildings were just rotting away.

2. Land in the four main cities was expensive, so houses were built upwards. Tenement flats were high, but cheap to build. The builders and landlords packed in as many families as possible to get multiple rents. This led to dark, closely built streets.

3. Land, water, gas and even the city dung heaps were often privately owned. Before the 1860s Town Councils didn't interfere much with the rights of private owners. There were few laws to protect the community from pollution and disease.

4. Town Councils often had little wish to improve things. Many people at the time believed that private owners should be left alone to do as they pleased with their property. Private profit was more important than public health.

5. It would be expensive to provide good housing, fresh water and clean streets. Many middle-class people did not want to pay high rates to improve the poor districts of town.

6. The slum dwellers themselves often made things worse. Many were ignorant and didn't realise the importance of personal hygiene and cleanliness.

WHY SHOULD I PAY RATES AND TAXES TO CLEAN UP THE POOR PARTS OF TOWN? THE PEOPLE WHO LIVE IN THE SLUMS SHOULD HELP THEMSELVES MORE. MY SLAUGHTER-HOUSE AND DUNG-YARD GIVE A LOT OF PEOPLE WELL PAID JOBS. IF YOU DON'T LIKE IT, YOU CAN JUST MOVE AWAY.... I HAVE A RIGHT TO MAKE A LIVING AS I PLEASE!

IF CHOLERA BREAKS OUT IN THE SLUMS, IT WILL SPREAD THROUGH THE WHOLE CITY. GIVE THE POOR CLEAN WATER AND SEWERS AND WE MAKE THE CITY SAFER FOR US ALL. PUBLIC HEALTH IS MORE IMPORTANT THAN PRIVATE PROFIT. NO FACTORY OR BUSINESS SHOULD BE ALLOWED TO POLLUTE THE STREETS. THE TOWN COUNCIL SHOULD SEE TO THIS....!

SOURCE S: Public Health or Private Profit?

It is fifty years since the water companies began in this town. Their product is stale and only to be got in half the streets in the city. They do not have to lay pipes where it does not pay them to do so. The poorer districts, where the people cannot afford the high water charges, are left without water. . .

SOURCE R: Glasgow doctor's report, 1853

Questions

1. Who would you blame for the slums in Scotland's cities at this time? Give reasons for your answer.

2. (a) According to Source R, why was much of Glasgow 'without water'?
   (b) How would this lack of water affect the health of the city?

3. Which of the two men in Source S is giving the more sensible view, in your opinion?

A new broom

BY THE 1860s, MANY people agreed that something had to be done about the poor state of the slum areas. More people realised then public health was in everybody's best interest. Most people accepted that it also had to be paid for.

The Town Councils began to take responsibility to improve things. City Improvement Acts were passed which gave Councils the power to close and demolish slums. A limit was put on the number who could sleep in a slum-building. The number allowed was shown on a metal ticket hung over the door. 'Ticketed' houses were inspected every night by the police who fined 'extra' dwellers.

Councils could now plan new, wider streets in poor parts of town. Water, gas and rubbish collection came under Council control. Water pipes and sewers were built under the streets to most homes. Work-places and housing began to be kept apart.

> The buildings No. 1 and No. 2 Rhind's Court, belonging to Mr. D. G. Cattenach, advocate, are all unfit for human habitation. By Order of the Town Council, these buildings shall be shut up, closed and not used as dwelling places after this date . . .

SOURCE T: Public Health Committee, Aberdeen Town Council Minutes, 1884

> The business of a Blood Boiler, Bone Boiler, Tanner, Slaughterer of Cattle, Horses or any animal, Soap Boiler, Skinner, Tallow Melter, Tripe Boiler or any other business injurious to the public health, shall not be newly built in any place within the Burgh of Aberdeen.

SOURCE U: Public Health Committee, Aberdeen Town Council Minutes, 1884

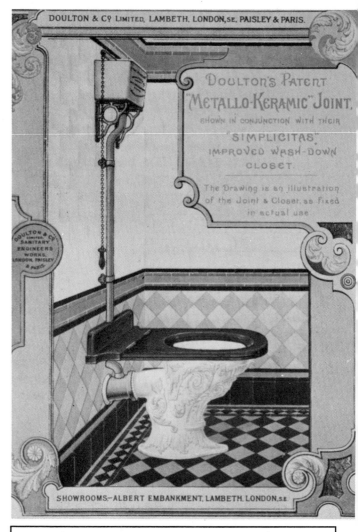

DOULTON & C? LIMITED, LAMBETH, LONDON, SE. PAISLEY & PARIS.

DOULTON'S PATENT "METALLO-KERAMIC" JOINT, SHOWN IN CONJUNCTION WITH THEIR "SIMPLICITAS" IMPROVED WASH-DOWN CLOSET.

The Drawing is an illustration of the Joint & Closet, as fixed in actual use.

DOULTON & C? LIMITED SANITARY ENGINEERS WORKS, LONDON, PAISLEY & PARIS.

SHOWROOMS—ALBERT EMBANKMENT, LAMBETH, LONDON, SE.

SOURCE V: Advertisement for a water-closet

Things to Do

1. (a) Many slum dwellers were not happy when their homes were closed, as described in Source T. Suggest a reason why this was so.
   (b) Who else would not be happy at the closure of these buildings?

2. Read Source U. Where would businesses like these have to go after 1884?

3. What would a Town Council have to provide, before the invention in Source V could be used?

Housing the homeless

POOR HOUSING was a problem in all of Scotland's cities throughout the period 1830 to 1930. City Councils demolished slums, but they had little money to build new homes. Clearing slum tenements often meant that overcrowding and homelessness got worse. Some homeless people ended up in the Model Lodging Houses. These were built by Town Councils after the 1870s. A bed for the night cost threepence. A bath and a Bible lecture came free. The 'modellers' were often run with very strict discipline and were inspected every night by the police.

There were some attempts to improve the homes of the poor. The first council-owned house was built in Glasgow in 1890. The Workmen's Dwellings Company, a charity, had built excellent homes for 2000 people by 1903. But with a million people in Glasgow, many were still living in slums in 1930.

SOURCE W: Crumbling slums in the 1930s

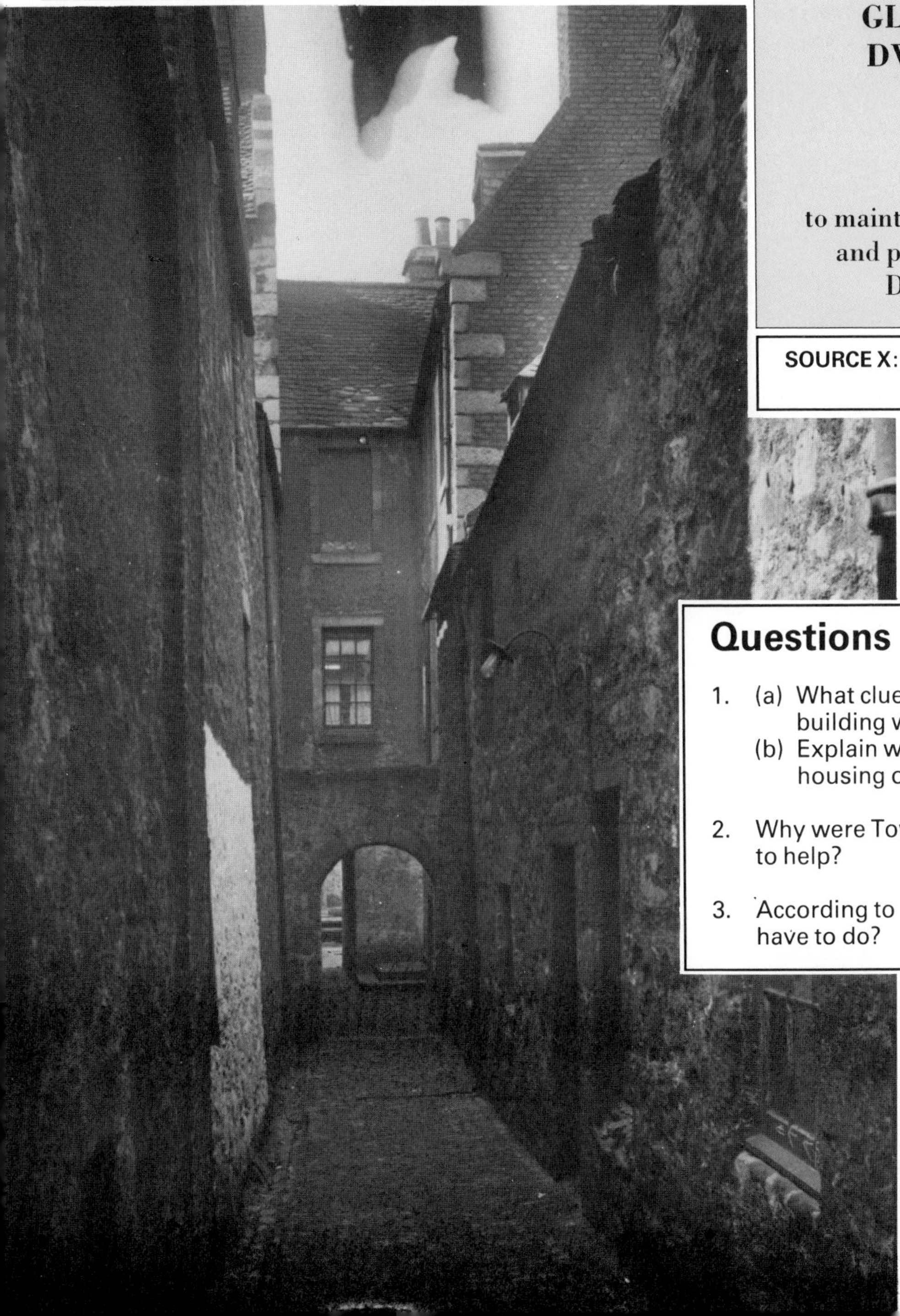

REQUIRED BY THE GLASGOW WORKMEN'S DWELLINGS COMPANY

A Sober and Watchful
Caretaker,

to maintain the Property of the company and press against the habits of Filth, Disorder and Drunkenness.

SOURCE X: Job advertisement for tenement caretaker, 1901

Questions

1. (a) What clue in Source W tells you that this building was to be closed?
   (b) Explain why attempts to improve city housing often made things worse.

2. Why were Town Councils unable to do more to help?

3. According to Source X, what did a caretaker have to do?

Civic pride

BY 1900, CITY LIFE for many Scots was cleaner and healthier than it had ever been. Clean water, street lights, surfaced roads and sewers had become commonplace. Hazards to public health were slowly being removed.

The wealthy middle classes moved out to new suburbs on the city edge. Here they lived in large, comfortable houses with gardens and servants.

Working people who had regular jobs were now able to save money to buy a better home in one of the quality tenements from building companies like McTaggarts. These apartments often had bathrooms, hot and cold water and separate water-closets.

Many people grew proud of their town or city. Councils built grand Town Halls to show off their wealth and their civic pride. It was easy to forget that there were still thousands living in slums.

SOURCE Y: Suburbs on the city edge, Glasgow, 1880

Things to Investigate

1. Have a look at the houses in your area. Are there any that look as if they were built in the period 1830 – 1930?
   What clues are there to tell you the age of these houses?
   What words best describe these houses?

2. Go to your public library. Ask to see the Ordnance Survey Map for your area in 1868 and 1901. (Years when early O.S. maps were published.)
   Compare this map with what exists in your area today.
   Make a list of the changes you can see.
   Try to think why these changes took place.

CHAPTER SIX
Towards Democracy

No votes for the poor

IN 1830 BRITAIN was ruled by a few rich landowners. They controlled the Government. Parliament only made laws to suit these powerful men. Very few Scots were allowed to vote in elections.

You had to be rich or powerful or own property to vote in Scotland. In the towns, a small group of burgh councillors chose the Member of Parliament. In country areas, important landlords decided who would represent the county at Westminster. In Scotland in 1830 only 4289 men had the vote.

In county elections the voting was done openly, in public, often at the local Market Cross, so everyone knew who you voted for. There was a lot of bribery and corruption.

The MPs were not divided fairly between different areas in Scotland. For example, Anstruther in Fife had been a thriving place in the Middle Ages, but by 1830 it was just a small village. Yet it had as much say in choosing the Government as Glasgow, the largest and wealthiest city in the land. New industrial towns like Paisley, which had 70 000 inhabitants, had no MP at all.

Factory towns had few MPs and almost no voters. The Government wasn't interested in them. It ignored the terrible conditions these towns were in by 1830.

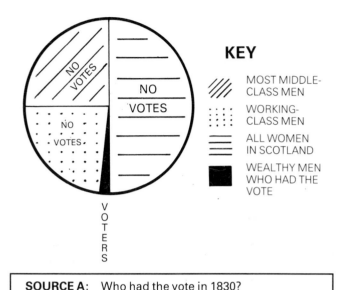

KEY

///// MOST MIDDLE-CLASS MEN

::::: WORKING-CLASS MEN

≡ ALL WOMEN IN SCOTLAND

■ WEALTHY MEN WHO HAD THE VOTE

SOURCE A:	Who had the vote in 1830?

Questions

1. What kinds of people had the vote in Scotland in 1830?

2. Why was voting in public a bad idea?

3. Why do you think factory towns like Paisley had no MP?

4. Was Scotland a democratic country in 1830? Give as many reasons as you can to explain your opinion.

The Scottish Reform Act, 1832

EFFECTS OF A STRIKE

UPON THE CAPITALIST   AND   UPON THE WORKING MAN.

SOURCE B: *Punch* cartoon showing lives of the rich and poor, 1839

IN THE YEARS 1830 and 1831 there were huge protest marches in Scotland. The marchers were protesting at the unfair way in which the Government was elected. They hoped they would get the vote and Britain would become a real democracy.

Many working people from the factory towns took part in these marches. They wanted to vote for a Government that would take an interest in them. They hoped it would pass laws to improve their poor living and working conditions.

There were great celebrations across Scotland in 1832 when the Government finally agreed to reform the voting laws.

The 1832 Scottish Reform Act increased the number of voters to over 65 000. It gave the vote to many middle-class Scots such as shopkeepers in the towns and farmers in the countryside.

However, the Act did not give the vote to working-class men and women. They still had no power to improve their living and working conditions.

SCOTTISH REFORM ACT 1832

The vote shall be given to:
* Men who own a town house valued at £10.
* Men who own a country house valued at £10.
* Men who rent a country house for £50 a year.

The number of voters in Scotland shall increase from 4200 to 65 000.

There shall be eight more Scottish MPs to represent the growing factory towns.

SOURCE C: Scottish Reform Act, 1832

Questions

1. (a) Look at Source B.
        Was the artist on the side of the rich man or the working people? What evidence in the picture tells you this?
    (b) Explain why getting the vote was so important to working people like those shown in Source B.

2. Study Source C. Which of these groups got the vote in 1832?

    People who owned a town house as well as a country house.
    Men and women who were quite well off.
    Men who were quite wealthy property owners or tenants.
    65 000 men who lived where the Government told them to.

3. Some historians claim that Britain became a democracy in 1832 because of the Reform Act. Do you agree?

The People's Charter

*W*ORKING PEOPLE were bitterly disappointed by the Reform Act. All over Britain they banded together in groups to fight for more changes in the voting laws.

Officials in London and Parliament drew up a list of demands. They called this list The People's Charter. People who supported these demands became known as Chartists. They decided to organise a National Petition which they would present to Parliament in London. The Chartists believed that if enough people signed the petition the Government would have to give in and grant their demands.

The Chartist leaders wanted to get their campaign off to a good start to show how many people supported them. They gathered in Glasgow where they knew there were thousands of bitter factory workers who wanted the vote. The first great Chartist meeting was held on Glasgow Green on 21 May, 1838.

THE
Chartist Circular.

'FOR A NATION TO LOVE LIBERTY, IT IS SUFFICIENT THAT SHE KNOWS IT; AND TO BE FREE, IT IS SUFFICIENT THAT SHE WILLS IT.'
M. De La Fayette.

Universal Suffrage, Annual Parliaments, Vote by Ballot, No Property Qualifications, Payment of Members, & Equal Electoral Districts.

| No. 2. | GLASGOW, SATURDAY, SEPT. 28, 1839. | PRICE ONE-HALFPENNY. |

SOURCE D: Front page of a Scottish Chartist newspaper

A vast crowd of over 200 000 gathered on Glasgow Green to support the National Charter yesterday. Forty-three brass bands and 300 banners led this peaceful demonstration.

SOURCE E: Glasgow newspaper report, May 1838

A group of around 30 000 unemployed hand-loom weavers has met in protest in Glasgow. Local troops and militia were held in readiness in case of a riot or damage to property.

SOURCE F: London newspaper report, May 1838

Questions

1. Study Source D.
   Find and list the six demands of the Chartists.
   Use a dictionary to help you match these demands with the correct meanings listed below.
   – All men to have the vote.
   – Voting to be secret.
   – MPs to be not only rich property owners.
   – Elections every year.
   – MPs to be paid.
   – Each MP to represent an area of equal population.

2. Look at the two reports of the first Chartist meeting (Sources E and F).
   Which report came from:
   (a) a Chartist newspaper?
   (b) a newspaper which distrusted the Government?

3. Why do you think the Government feared the Chartists?

4. Which of the six Chartist demands are part of our modern voting system?

Towards a better Scotland

THOUSANDS of Scots became Chartists in the 1830s and 1840s. There were over 100 Chartist branches in Scotland, collecting signatures for the Great Petition to Parliament. There were over 50 Chartist newspapers, spreading their message. But many Scottish Chartists wanted more than the vote.

Some set up schools to give their children a 'Chartist education'. There were Chartist shops where unemployed and poorly paid workers could buy good food at prices they could afford. There were Chartist Christians who built churches for factory workers. Getting the vote was just the first step towards giving the ordinary people of Scotland a better life.

SOURCE I: Scottish Chartist demands, 1841

SOURCE G: Map showing Chartist branches in Scotland in 1840

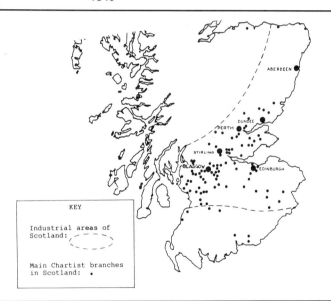

KEY

Industrial areas of Scotland: - - -

Main Chartist branches in Scotland: •

Scottish Chartists Unite!

Let the millions who labour
Unite heart and hand
And the Charter will soon
Be the law of the land!

SOURCE J: Chartist banner

SOURCE H: The Chartist Co-operative Store, Hawick, 1839

THE CHARTIST STORE

PLOUGH A

Questions

1. Why do you think Chartism was popular in the area shown in Source G?

2. What would be taught at a Chartist school?

3. Why were Chartist food stores like the one in Source H necessary?

4. Which of the Chartists' social demands in Source I eventually came about?

Moral and physical force

MANY CHARTISTS thought that their demands were reasonable. They believed the Government would listen to their arguments, and that no violence would be needed to get the vote. These Moral Force Chartists expected to have the same success as the middle class had in 1832 in the Reform campaign.

However, the Government was not ready to give the vote to working people. They viewed the poor as an ignorant 'mob', a 'rabble' that was not fit to share in the serious business of running the country. The first Petition, with a million names, was presented to Parliament in 1839. It was ignored. Other Chartist petitions were organised in 1842 and 1848, with no success.

Some Chartists could bear their poverty no longer. They tried to use force to get their demands. These Physical Force Chartists were involved in strikes and riots. There was talk of a revolution.

The Government acted quickly. Police forces were set up in every major town. Orders to arrest leading Chartists were sent by the new electric telegraph. Troops were sent to stop riots on the railway system. After 1848 Chartism fizzled out.

Chartist Disturbance

An ugly crowd collected on Glasgow Green, claiming that they were starving, and proceeded to march through the main streets of the city, entering and looting shops as they went.

The police were unable to cope, so the military were called in to disperse the rioters . . . the militia were forced to fire into the crowd, killing six and wounding several others. Sixty-four people were arrested after the riots and twenty were convicted and sentenced.

SOURCE L: Newspaper report, 16 March, 1848

A PHYSICAL FORCE CHARTIST ARMING FOR THE FIGHT.

SOURCE K: A Physical Force Chartist arming for the fight, *Punch* cartoon

Questions

1. Look at Source K.
   How has the cartoonist tried to make a fool of the Chartist?

2. (a) Read Source L. What clues in the report suggest that the writer was against Chartism?
   (b) Is there any evidence in the report which proves that these rioters were Chartists?
   How would you explain the headline given to this article?

Votes for some

THE MAIN AIM of the Chartists was to get the vote for all men, but they failed to get this in the 1840s. The wealthy upper and middle classes, who had the vote, saw no reason to share their power. The idea of poor working-class men taking part in electing the Government was too new.

In 1867 a Second Reform Act was passed by Parliament. It greatly increased the number of voters. Many of these new voters were quite ordinary working men who lived in towns. An Act in 1884 gave male country workers the vote. From 1872 onwards, voting was done in secret, using a ballot box, so no-one could see how you had voted.

But people still did not have an automatic right to vote. You still had to own or rent a house worth a certain value. It was only in 1918 that all men over 21 gained the vote as a basic right, and even then you had to be male to be an elector.

SOURCE M:
How many voters in Scotland?

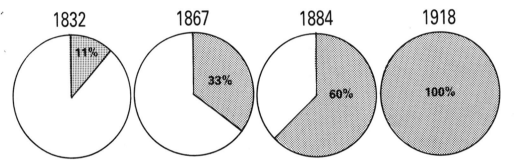

1832 — 11%

1867 — 33%

1884 — 60%

1918 — 100%

PERCENTAGE OF ADULT MALE SCOTS WHO HAD THE VOTE

SOURCE N:
Working men voting at a General Election

Questions

1. According to Source M, which Act gave the vote to most Scots?

2. Study Source N. It shows working men voting in a General Election. Using what you have read above, and what you can see in the source, choose the date of this picture from the list below.
   Possible dates: 1830; 1868; 1874; 1884; 1918.

3. What kinds of men would not have had the vote in the years between 1884 and 1918?

Women: second class citizens

IT WAS A MAN'S world in the nineteenth century. Women took little part in governing the country or running its trade and industry. Men were completely in charge of those things that were considered to be 'important'. Most men just laughed at the thought that women should be treated as equals and given the vote.

Middle-class women were expected to be good wives, mothers and home-builders. Often they had been given little real education. They were only trained in skills like etiquette and dancing that would help them catch a better husband.

Poorer women were often treated very badly, working long hours for low wages. Usually they did cold, unpleasant jobs which men preferred not to do, like gutting fish. Some women, like seamstresses, were paid starvation wages. To feed their families, these women had to accept any work they could get.

Women had few legal rights, even in their own family lives where their husband was master of the house. There was nothing women could do to change this state of affairs, as they had no vote.

Female Parliament.

SOURCE O: A Female Parliament (cartoon)

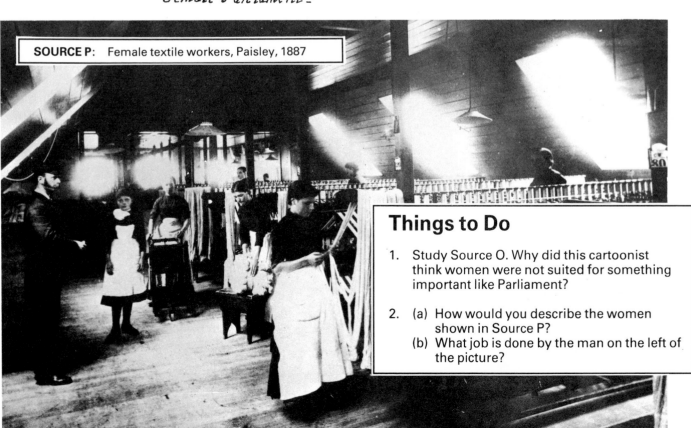

SOURCE P: Female textile workers, Paisley, 1887

Things to Do

1. Study Source O. Why did this cartoonist think women were not suited for something important like Parliament?

2. (a) How would you describe the women shown in Source P?
   (b) What job is done by the man on the left of the picture?

The new woman

AFTER 1860 MANY middle-class women began to get better education. A growing number of girls now studied at college and university. Some began to hold responsible jobs, in professions such as teaching and medicine. These women were often bitter at the way they were treated by men.

Changes in the voting laws after 1867 made them especially angry. Ordinary working men now had the vote. It was possible for a man to vote even if he was quite ignorant, just because he was a man. An intelligent woman with a deep knowledge of politics had no say in choosing the Government, just because she was a woman.

In the late 1860s, a number of women began to fight for the right to vote. 'Suffrage' is an old word meaning a vote, so they called themselves 'Suffragists'. Like the Chartists before them, they collected signatures on a petition and tried to persuade MPs to support them.

SOURCE Q:
Women's Movement poster

What a Woman may be, and yet not have the Vote

MAYOR NURSE MOTHER DOCTOR or TEACHER FACTORY HAND

What a Man may have been, & yet not lose the Vote

CONVICT LUNATIC Proprietor of white Slaves Unfit for Service DRUNKARD

Their coachmen, their gardeners, the very labourers on their estate have votes, while the mistress who employs and pays them is not considered competent to give this simple vote.

SOURCE R: Popular magazine, 1898

Few women have a real interest in politics that goes beyond the surface appearance of their candidate. How many of these giddy creatures will know how to exercise the great power of election wisely?

SOURCE S: Popular magazine, 1899

By the 1890s thousands of women, and some famous men of the time, belonged to the Suffragist movement. The National Union of Women's Suffrage Societies held massive demonstrations in London. It seemed only a matter of time before women were given the vote and equality with men.

Questions

1. Why were many women increasingly angry in the late nineteenth century? Use the information in Source Q to develop your answer.

2. (a) In your own words, explain the points being made in Sources R and S.
   (b) Which of these sources probably came from a Suffragist magazine?

Deeds not words

BY 1900 MANY MEN agreed with the Suffragists, but women still had no vote. Some women believed that more violent tactics were needed to force the Government into action. In 1903 they formed the Women's Social and Political Union, with the motto 'Deeds not Words'.

In 1906, the leaders of the WSPU were arrested and sent to prison for making a protest in Parliament. These Suffragettes, as they were called, began to plan a shock campaign throughout the country. For the next eight years the Suffragettes damaged public buildings, set fire to letter-boxes and painted slogans on walls. At Moray Golf Club in Lossiemouth in 1913 the Prime Minister, Henry Asquith, was seriously assaulted by two young women.

This violence did not help. Many people of both sexes agreed with Asquith who felt that these lawless Suffragettes could not be trusted with the vote.

In the summer of 1914 Britain was dragged into the First World War. The leaders of the Suffragettes gave up their struggle for the vote. They turned their energies to the war effort. At first women helped by raising funds and setting up hospitals for the wounded. Later, they took on all kinds of jobs to release men for the army.

By 1918 women had worked four long years to help win the war. Even Asquith felt that these women deserved a reward from the nation. In 1918 women over the age of 30 years were given the vote.

By 1928 all women over 21 could take part in a General Election. Now all adult citizens had a chance to elect the Government. Britain had finally become a fully democratic country.

SOURCE T: National Service poster, 1916

NATIONAL  SERVICE   W/₃₃

10,000 Women Wanted For Farm Work

A FREE OUTFIT, high boots, breeches, overall and hat.

MAINTENANCE during training.

TRAVELLING expenses in connection with the work.

WAGES 18/- per week, or the district rate, whichever is the higher.

MAINTENANCE during terms of unemployment up to four weeks.

HOUSING personally inspected and approved by the Women's War Agricultural Committee in each County.

WORK on carefully selected farms.

PROMOTION. good work rewarded by promotion and higher pay.

AFTER THE WAR. special facilities for settlement at home or overseas.

DON'T DELAY ENROL TO-DAY

Application forms may be had at all Post Offices & Employment Exchanges.

DIRECTOR GENERAL OF NATIONAL SERVICE.
ST. ERMINS, S.W. 1.

Questions

1. (a) Read Source T. Why were so many women needed for farm work?
   (b) What kind of women do you think this poster was aimed at?

2. Explain why Britain was a democratic country only after 1928.

Things to Investigate

1. Visit your local library and look at the Electoral Roll for your street or area. How many people in your street or area can vote? How many of these would be entitled to vote if the year was:
   (a) 1830
   (b) 1900
   (c) 1918?

2. Look at extracts 6–8 of the Scottish Film Council video *A Century of Change*. What sort of people are demonstrating in these films? What are they demanding? Either individually, or in groups, try to find out more about these people.

CHAPTER SEVEN
Schools
Early schools

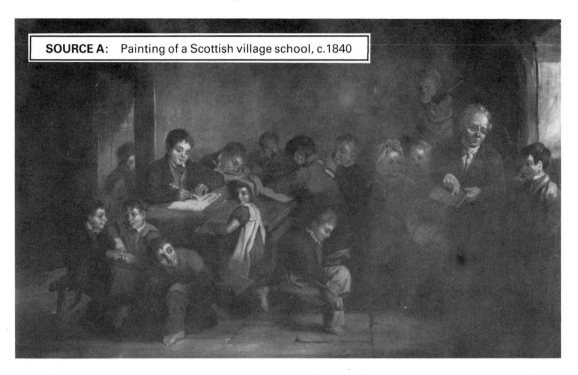

SOURCE A: Painting of a Scottish village school, c.1840

IN THE EARLY nineteenth century many Scottish children were regularly employed in factories, workshops, and on farms.

Many poor parents of numerous families are forced to employ their children at a very early age; we often find young children employed in spinning mills, sent there by their parents before they have been a few months at school.

SOURCE B: New Statistical Account, Perth, 1837

The schoolroom at Falkirk parish school is eighteen feet square. It holds one hundred and ten regular attenders.

SOURCE C: New Statistical Account, Falkirk, 1845

They seldom stayed long at school. There was no law to make parents send their children to school.

The Factory Act of 1833 said that children working in factories were supposed to have two hours of lessons each day, but often this did not happen. Government inspectors seldom checked up to see if the law was being carried out.

Questions and Things to Do

1. Look at Source A. What differences do you notice between this classroom and a modern classroom?

2. Why did so few children attend school in the 1830s?

3. Read Source C. Measure out a space 18 feet square in your history classroom.
   How many pupils are seated in a space that size nowadays?

Types of schools

THERE WERE many types of schools in Scotland at this time. In country areas, many village schools gave a good education at times of the year when pupils could be spared from farm work. But few schools had qualified teachers and some buildings were badly run down.

> *The school is a wretched building, the roof falling in, the walls stained green with damp, the desks old and frail, one window broken and stuffed with rags . . .*

SOURCE D: Report on Garcunnock Parish School, 1867

In the growing towns, free 'ragged' schools were opened to teach the children of the poorest families. Only the rich could afford a proper full-time education at a grammar school or an academy.

In the main cities of Scotland many children lived a life of crime on the streets.

By 1860 many reform schools had been set up. These schools tried to give young offenders training for a job and helped them to keep out of trouble.

No.	Name.	Age.	Court before which Convicted.	Offence.	Endurance of Reformatory Sentence.	Number of Convictions.	Parentage.	Date of Admission.
								1857.
1	A	13	Police Court,	Theft of Keys, &c.,	4 years,	First,	Mother, Illegitimate	3d April.
2	B	10	Police Court,	Theft of Gls. Bottles,	5 years,	First,	Father, Stepmother	3d April.
3	C	10	Police Court,	Theft of Gls. Bottles,	5 years,	First,	Father only,	3d April.
4	D	15½	Sheriff Court	Theft of Lead, &c.	2 years,	Fifth,	Father, Mother,	6th April.
5	E	12	Police Court,	Theft of Gls. Bottles,	5 years,	First,	Mother, deserted by Father,	17th April.
6	F	10	Police Court,	Theft of Lead, &c.	5 years,	Fifth,	Father, Mother,	17th April.
7	G	13	Police Court,	Theft of Lead, &c.,	5 years,	Third,	Father only,	17th April
8	H	11	Police Court,	Theft of Tallow,	5 years,	First,	Mother, Stepfather,	15th May.
9	I	15	Police Court,	Theft of Bread,	3 years,	First,	Mother, Stepfather,	20th May.
10	J	15	Police Court,	Theft of Tub, &c.,	3 years,	Second,	Father only,	20th May.
11	K	13	Sheriff Court,	Theft of Money,	2 years,	Second,	Mother, Husband, Illegitimate	19th June.
12	L	10	Police Court,	Theft of Gls. Bottles,	5 years,	First,	Father, Mother,	17th Aug.
13	M	10	Police Court,	Theft of Gls. Bottles,	5 years,	First,	Father, Mother,	17th Aug.
14	N	10	Police Court,	Theft of 2 Whips,	5 years,	First,	Mother, deserted by Father,	11th Sept.
15	O	14	Sheriff Court,	Theft of Potatoes,	2 years,	Fourth,	Father, Mother,	26th Sept.
16	P	14	Sheriff Court,	Theft of Potatoes,	2 years,	Third,	Mother, Widow,	26th Sept.
17	Q	13	Police Court,	Theft of a Watch,	3 years,	First,	Father, Mother,	11th Dec.
18	R	14	Police Court,	Theft of Apples,	3 years,	First,	deserted by Father, Mother,	24th Dec.
19	S	13	Sheriff Court,	Theft of Money,	2 years,	First,	Father, Mother.	28th Dec.

SOURCE E: Class-list of pupils at a reform school, 1857

DR. GUTHRIE'S RAGGED SCHOOL This school is FREE to all children.

WEST BOW, EDINBURGH — 1852

Questions

1. Imagine you were a child at the school in Source D. Describe your classroom and how you feel as you attend your lessons.

2. (a) What was the main cause of becoming a reform school pupil according to Source E?
   (b) Why do you think people like Dr Guthrie wanted to help the children of poor families?

Lessons

SOURCE F: Visitors watching a display at Robert Owen's school in New Lanark

IN MOST SMALL Scottish schools, the main subjects taught were the '3 Rs' – reading, writing, arithmetic (reading, 'riting and 'rithmetic) and Bible study. Robert Owen's model school at New Lanark was the first to teach a wide range of subjects, such as history, nature study, singing and dancing. It became world famous.

Many children learned to read the Bible at a Sunday school. Others went to charity schools where for a penny a day they learned to read, write and do simple arithmetic.

> The subjects to be taught at the Aberdeen Grammar School this term, 1852, are Latin, Greek and ancient geography.

SOURCE G: *Aberdeen Almanack*, 1852

> The subjects taught at Pollockshaws Industrial School this year;
> Carpentry, Shoe-making, Tailoring, Wood-splitting, Knitting, Sewing, Darning, Cookery, Baking, Washing, Scrubbing.

SOURCE H: Headteacher's report, Glasgow, 1859

After 1850 industrial schools were set up in towns to teach older children practical subjects like cookery and carpentry.

Grammar schools and academies taught more book-based subjects like history, English and languages.

Things to Do

1. Copy the chart below, filling in the different subjects which would be taught at each school.

School	Subjects
Small village school Robert Owen's school Sunday schools Charity schools Grammar schools Industrial schools	

2. Which of these schools do you think would have given you the best education? Give a reason for your answer.

3. What clues are there in Source F to tell you what was taught at New Lanark?

4. What kinds of pupils would you have expected to find at:
   (a) Aberdeen Grammar School?
   (b) Pollockshaws School?

School attendance

SOURCE I: Getting to school in Glenbuchat, c.1900

SCHOOL ATTENDANCE varied from place to place in the mid-nineteenth century. It often depended on the weather and the time of year. In the more remote areas of Scotland, such as the Highlands and Islands, children were expected to walk long distances to school.

The attendance was very irregular during this week owing to very cold and stormy weather.

SOURCE J: Birsay School Logbook, Orkney, 1874

Not all parents in Scotland at this time wanted their children to go to school. Many kept their children working instead.

Despite the low rate of fees, it cannot be said that the people here are aware of the benefits of education.

SOURCE K: Kirkden School Logbook, Forfarshire, 1840

The parents, in general, are anxious to give education to their children. The number present in the school at the last examination was nearly 100, a large attendance considering the size of the parish.

SOURCE L: Eassie School Logbook, Forfarshire, 1842

Questions

1. What reasons are given in Sources I and J for low attendance at some schools?

2. (a) On what point do Sources K and L disagree?
    (b) Why is it surprising that these two sources give different views?
    (c) Which of these sources gives evidence to make its point?

The Government steps in

SOURCE M: A Board School in Aberdeen, 1885

IN THE 1870s, the Government decided that all children should get a basic education. Scotland was becoming a modern country. Its people needed to read and write so they could work in more skilled jobs.

The Scottish Education Act 1872

This new law said that all children aged between 5 and 13 had to go to school, but parents had to pay 2d or 3d a week for each child. Many poor families could not afford to pay this and so ignored the law.

In most areas a School Board was set up. Its job was to see that enough schools were built, that they were kept in good order and that houses were provided for the teachers. The Board kept a check on pupils' attendance, inspected the work done in each school and made sure the teachers were properly qualified.

Free Schools 1890

A law passed in 1890 made education free for 5–14-year-olds. This was elementary or primary education for all. After 1890 attendance at school improved.

Pupils still had to pay fees at secondary schools. Most children from poorer families left school once their primary days were over.

Questions

1. Why did some parents still not send their children to school after 1872?

2. Describe in your own words what a Board School looked like.

3. Make a list of the jobs the School Boards did. Use the sources in this chapter to say why School Boards were needed.

Examinations

SOURCE N: School leaver's certificate, Edinburgh, 1889

COMPULSORY attendance applied only to elementary schools. In the 1870s children normally left school at the age of twelve and went out to work. They would sit an examination before leaving and be awarded a leaver's certificate. This contained a list of the subjects which they had studied and passed.

> *3rd Nov.   Scholarship boys making little progress towards their exam. Strapped the class. Much pleased with the result.*

SOURCE O: Kincardineshire School Logbook, 1877

Sometimes the Government gave money to help run schools. The amount it gave depended on the school's exam results. A good school where pupils did well was more likely to get Government money than a school where standards were lower.

Questions

1. Which schools got Government money after 1872?

2. (a) According to Source N, which subjects were examined in schools in the 1890s?
   (b) What modern subjects were not examined then?
   (c) What word meaning 'pupil' is used in this source?

3. Suggest how the teacher who wrote Source O was paid.

4. How were children punished in Scottish schools at this time?

Caring for the kids

SOURCE P: Lauriston School, Edinburgh, c.1915

BY 1900 ALMOST ALL children in Scotland were attending elementary school. The Inspectors began to notice that many children were badly fed, poorly clothed and often had no shoes. Many children were sickly and not very clean.

In 1907 the Liberal Government decided that school dinners should be given to children who needed them. School Boards were also told to check on standards of hygiene, give boots and clothing to the poorest children, and give all pupils regular medical inspections.

Dinners supplied to 120 children today. The number is rising weekly . . . mostly children from army families.

SOURCE Q: School Log, Edinburgh, November 1914

Questions

1. (a) Look at Source P. Why do you think these boys have had their hair cut so short?
   (b) List the things in this picture that could have been provided by the School Board.

2. Look at the date of Source Q. Suggest a reason why the number of army children needing free school dinners had suddenly gone up.

3. Which of the 1907 improvements are still part of school life today?

Nursery schools

AFTER 1918 MORE women began to go out to work. A few nursery schools were opened by the Government in the 1920s. There was always a long waiting list for these. Parents who could afford it sent their under-fives to private nurseries.

SOURCE R: Ready for lunch at Dumbiedykes Day Nursery, Edinburgh, 1924

Free Secondary Education

BY THE 1918 Education Act, schools came under the control of local councils. Councils were also now in charge of the many Catholic schools which had developed, mainly in the west of Scotland.

After 1918 more children began to stay on at school after the age of 14. The Government set up free secondary schools. Senior Secondaries were for those 12–17-year-olds who passed the qualifying entrance exam. Junior Secondaries were for those who failed the 'qually'.

Secondary classes were very large because it was expensive to employ well-qualified teachers in every subject. Classes were often as big as 55. Most of the first secondary schools were single sex: boys were taught woodwork, physics and football; girls were taught cookery, sewing and childcare.

Pupils who did well at a Senior Secondary had the chance to go on and study for a degree at one of Scotland's four ancient universities. Pupils at a Junior Secondary went straight to work when they left school.

Questions

1. What evidence in Source R tells you that nursery schools were expensive to run?

2. Explain why secondary classes were so large compared with today?

Schools in the Highands

BY 1900 THE ENGLISH language was being used in Highland schools instead of Gaelic. A school inspector said in 1899, 'The Gaelic language is beautiful, but the people do not want it.' However, the 1918 Education Act said that both languages had to be taught in Gaelic-speaking areas. This was to make sure that the Scots did not lose an important part of their heritage.

Question

1. Why did the School Inspectors believe Gaelic was important to schools in the Highlands?

Things to Investigate

1. Find out if your school has a log book. See how far back it goes. Choose a period you are interested in and read the log entries for those years.

   Make notes of anything interesting you find, under the headings Buildings, Pupils and Classes, Teachers and Subjects, Holidays and Daily Life.

2. Look at extracts 7–13 of Section 2 of the Scottish Film Council video *A Century of Change*. In small groups, discuss the following points;
   (a) Old and new ways of teaching. How are they different? Which are better?
   (b) Separate education for girls and boys. What are the good points and bad points of this? Why have most schools given up this idea?
   (c) Health provision in schools. How has this changed over the years?

Finding out the facts

How do we know about Scotland in the years between 1830 and 1930? There are many types of sources which give us information about the past.

Some of the most useful sources are official. For example, after 1801, the Government took a Census or head count every ten years, so we have reliable facts from then on. Other official sources in this book include council minutes, police reports and school log-books.

Another important source of information is The New Statistical Account of Scotland. In 1832 it was decided to ask every parish minister to write a report, giving details of the history, population, economy and industries in his area. The NSA is a valuable and fascinating source for Scotland in the 1830s and 1840s.

Newspapers and magazines contain not only written articles, but drawings, cartoons and advertisements which illustrate the period. Maps and engravings survive from the first half of the century. By the 1860s, photography had begun to give an accurate visual record of life in Scotland.

Things to Investigate

1. Look back through this book, noting sources that come from the NSA.

   Make a list of the things mentioned in these extracts.

2. Ask at your school or local library to see the NSA report on your area.
   (a) What has changed in your area since the 1830s?
   (b) Has anything survived down to the present day?

3. Go back through the book. Make a list of the many different kinds of source that are used in this book.